D1627142

The Brothers
Grimm

Other titles in the Inventors and Creators series include:

The Brothers Grimm

Raymond H. Miller

KIDHAVEN PRESS
An imprint of Thomson Gale, a part of The Thomson Corporation

THOMSON

GALE

Detroit • New York • San Francisco • San Diego • New Haven, Conn. • Waterville, Maine • London • Munich

For more information, contact
KidHaven Press
27500 Drake Rd.
Farmington Hills, MI 48331-3535
Or you can visit our Internet site at http://www.gale.com

LIBRARY OF CONGRESS CATALOGING-IN-PUBLICATION DATA

Miller, Raymond H., 1967–
The Brothers Grimm / by Raymond H. Miller.
   p. cm. — (Inventors and creators)
Includes bibliographical references and index.
Contents: Once upon a time—Leaving home—Grimm's Fairy Tales—A lasting legacy.
ISBN 0-7377-3157-5 (alk. paper)
   1. Grimm, Jacob, 1785–1863—Juvenile literature. 2. Grimm, Wilhelm, 1786–1859—Juvenile literature. 3. Philologists—Germany—Biography—Juvenile literature. 4. Kinder- und Hausmärchen—Juvenile literature. I. Title. II. Series.
PD63.M55 2005
830.9'2243—dc22
                                                     2005004557

Contents

Chapter One

Once Upon a Time

Jacob Ludwig Carl Grimm was born on January 4, 1785, to Philipp and Dorothea Zimmer Grimm. Jacob's brother, Wilhelm Carl Grimm, was born thirteen months later on February 24, 1786. Philipp and Dorothea had three more sons, Carl, Ferdinand, and Ludwig, and a daughter named Charlotte. The family would have been larger, but three other sons died before their first birthday. The entire family was very close, but Jacob and Wilhelm enjoyed a special bond. The two boys did nearly everything together, from waking up at the same time and eating meals together to playing side by side all day and going to bed at the same time.

The Grimms were an upper middle-class family who lived in the kingdom of Hessen-Kassel. It was one of the many independent territories that made up Germany in the late 18th century. Philipp Grimm earned a good living as a lawyer and the town clerk in the village of Hanau. He often wore a uniform around the house and encouraged the children to respond to him in military fashion. This was done to teach them discipline. The Grimms were **Hessians**, a proud group of people who valued the importance of tradition and heritage. Philipp's father and grandfather had been respected clergymen in Hessen-Kassel, so Philipp made sure that religion was a

This monument to Jacob and Wilhelm Grimm stands in front of the town hall in Hanau, Germany, where the brothers were born.

central part of the children's lives. The entire family faithfully attended church each week. After hearing his grandfather preach, Jacob would sometimes stand on a stool and imitate him in a lively fashion.

Dorothea Grimm was a kind woman who was adored by Jacob, Wilhelm, and the rest of the children. But in those days, it was common for the mother to supervise the daily affairs of the household while servants raised the children. One of the Grimm family's two servants, a **nursemaid** named Gretchen, was a favorite of Jacob and Wilhelm's. She occasionally sneaked them bread and cheese and told them old Hessian stories, which they found fascinating.

Early Education

Playing an even greater role in raising Jacob and Wilhelm was their favorite aunt, Julianne Schlemmer. She was Philipp's older sister. Philipp invited Julianne to move in with the family, and she became the boys' first teacher. Like Philipp, she was firm with the children and had high expectations for them. She told them stories from the *Bible* and taught them how to read and write. Because she used a long pin to point forcefully to the letters on the pages of a wooden-covered spelling book, the book's pages quickly became filled with tiny holes. Jacob and Wilhelm also learned French from a tutor and studied dance with an instructor in Hanau.

In 1791, the family left Hanau and moved to the nearby town of Steinau. Philipp had been named the town **magistrate**, a government official who administered

The Brothers Grimm first heard fairy tales as children. Their lifelong fascination with such tales as "Sleeping Beauty" would earn them lasting literary fame.

the laws. Jacob was then six years old and Wilhelm was five. During the first few years at Steinau, Jacob and Wilhelm did not attend the local school. Instead, they learned from a private tutor who taught them in a special classroom set up inside their home. Their teacher, Herr Johann Georg Zinckban, was strict and old-fashioned. The brothers found the teacher's lessons incredibly boring.

A Magical Setting

Jacob and Wilhelm escaped the boredom of Herr Zinckban's lessons by finding excitement in and around

The old turreted house where Jacob and Wilhelm lived in Steinau inspired the boys' active imagination.

their Steinau home. The old house was every child's dream. There were chickens, cows, ducks, and horses to feed. They also loved playing with the lambs that wandered around the courtyard. Their house had a **turret**, or tower, from which the boys spied on guests. Surrounding their property was a large stone wall that was perfect for climbing.

The brothers had little trouble finding excitement beyond those walls. They were curious and were often on the search for interesting things to see and do. Many of their days were spent walking the rolling hills and exploring flowers, insects, and trees. One of their favorite places to play was on the banks of the Stadtborn River behind their house. There they made pretend boats out of leaves and turned broken tree twigs into waterwheels. The brothers also loved watching the many fascinating people of Steinau. An entertaining afternoon might include watching a woodsman chop and haul wood or a goose girl driving her flock through the sprawling fields.

The town of Steinau also offered excitement for young Jacob and Wilhelm. It had several castles, bell towers, and stone walls that dated from the medieval period. The boys were often allowed to walk into the center of

With its medieval stone walls and towers, Steinau Castle was an exciting place for the imaginative brothers to play.

town and play in the water of a moat surrounding one of the castles. In the fall they played war games, using acorns as soldiers. The pretend war often took place at the old city wall, where they used former guardhouses as forts. For pretend **artillery**, they stuck apples on the end of a stick, then catapulted them at a make-believe enemy.

Growing Up Fast

When Jacob was ten and Wilhelm was nine, the two boys learned that real war was not any fun. The people of France had grown tired of being ruled by the government of the king and started a revolutionary war. Because Germany borders France, the fight soon spread to many of the German kingdoms. Hessen-Kassel was soon caught in the middle. German and foreign soldiers were often seen walking the streets of Steinau. Napoléon Bonaparte, a French officer who later became emperor, was taking control of the French army and conquering parts of Europe. Napoléon had his eye on Germany and led his armies through Steinau. Before long, Dutch and Austrian soldiers made their way through the countryside to fight the French. Many of these soldiers were violent, and the brothers were forbidden to leave the house when they were nearby.

As Steinau magistrate, Philipp Grimm was called on to investigate many of the complaints townspeople had about the soldiers. As a result, he was away from home much of the time. During the Christmas holiday of 1795, he remained home for several weeks, though it was not under cheerful circumstances. He had become sick with

In the early nineteenth century, Napoléon marched his troops through Steinau during his campaign to conquer Germany.

pneumonia, causing him to lose his appetite and become extremely weak. The boys were happy when their father seemed to be recovering. Jacob, age eleven at the time, wrote an elegant letter to his grandfather about his father's health. "Our dear father is regaining his appetite and would like some of baker Schuko's special bread. Mother asks if you would be so good to send a small loaf. It must be freshly baked since Father cannot eat anything dry."[1] By the time Grandfather Zimmer could reply, however, Philipp's health took an unexpected turn for the worse. He died on January 10, 1796. Suddenly, Dorothea and her children were on their own and facing an uncertain future.

Chapter 2

Leaving Home

Dorothea Grimm had no income other than a small government pension from Philipp's job as magistrate. A family that was used to the comforts of middle class life quickly found out what it was like to be poor. Dorothea and her children were forced to leave their beloved Steinau home. They eventually moved into a house Dorothea could barely afford to buy. At just eleven and ten years old, Jacob and Wilhelm took a leading role in caring for their siblings by bathing, dressing, and sometimes disciplining them. Meanwhile, Dorothea worked most of the day tending to the family's livestock. She even butchered her own pigs and made sausage for the family to eat.

Jacob and Wilhelm's education in Steinau nearly came to an end when Dorothea could no longer afford to pay Herr Zinckban. Henrietta Zimmer, Dorothea's older sister, knew the boys had great potential and refused to let her nephews go uneducated. She offered to pay for Jacob and Wilhelm's education at Lyceum Fridericianum (also called the Gymnasium). The school was located in Kassel, which meant the boys would be living away from home for the first time. Even so, Dorothea knew they needed a better education. So in the fall of 1798, when Jacob was thirteen and Wilhelm was twelve, Dorothea sent them to Kassel on horse and carriage. Jacob consoled a sobbing Wilhelm as their coach carried them past the familiar sights of Steinau on their way out of town.

The boys stopped in the city of Frankfurt to break up the long journey. They were amazed at the sight of all the buildings and people of this large, modern city. While in Frankfurt, the boys stayed with a friend of Grandfather Zimmer. To cheer up the homesick boys, he took them to a small circus, where they saw elephants, monkeys, parrots, and tigers for the first time. They were thrilled. Once they

On the journey from Steinau to the Gymnasium in Kassel in 1798, the brothers spent time in the large city of Frankfurt.

finally arrived in Kassel, their coach carried them along a 3-mile-long avenue (4.8km) that led up a tall hill to Schloss Wilhelmshote, a sprawling palace where their aunt served as **lady-in-waiting** to the countess.

School Days

Jacob and Wilhelm did not live at the palace with their aunt. Instead, they shared a room in the house of a palace cook. Each day they walked down the hill to the Gymnasium to attend classes. The brothers loved to learn, but at first they did not like their new school. The Gymnasium was prestigious, and unlike Jacob and Wilhelm, most of the students were from very wealthy families. Jacob was offended when the teachers addressed them with the old-fashioned "Er" (he). The teachers called the other students by the more formal "Sie" (you).

As a rule, the school tested all new students before placing them in a class. Jacob tested in the lowest of the school's four classes. Wilhelm tested so poorly that he did not qualify for any of the classes. As a result, he was required to study with a tutor before finally being admitted to the school. Despite their slow start, both brothers quickly caught up to the other students. Even the teachers who were hard on the brothers before now praised them. Although doing well at the school, Jacob did not like the **curriculum**. He wrote at the time that the school "wasted much time with geography, natural history, anthropology, morals, physics, logic, and philosophy, while the instruction in . . . [literature] and history, which should be the soul of all education . . . was neglected."[2]

Choosing to study law, Jacob enrolled at the university in Marburg in 1802. The university's church is pictured.

Jacob and Wilhelm's classes and study time left them little time for leisure. Each day they spent six hours at school and another four hours with a French and Latin tutor. When they did get a break from their studies, they explored the streets of Kassel with friends. One of their favorite things to do was to visit bookstores and spend time reading poetry and fairy tales. Both brothers were also interested in art. They sketched objects in their room and even walked into town to draw interesting sights.

In the spring of 1802, Jacob had finished his studies at the Gymnasium and was accepted at the university in Marburg. This meant the brothers would be separated for the first time in their lives. Both were heartbroken when Jacob left for Marburg.

Turning Point

Though Jacob's true interest was in history and literature, he chose to study law at the university. According
to Jacob, he did this "because my father had been a
lawyer and because mother wanted it that way."[3] Classes
again kept him busy, which helped take his mind off

A favorite law professor of the brothers, Friedrich Karl von
Savigny was drawn to the young men's love of learning.

Wilhelm, who was suffering from respiratory problems back in Kassel. Mindful of his brother's poor health, Jacob was serious all the time, rarely laughing at the other students' stories. They began calling him the "old man." However, his attitude improved when Wilhelm returned to good health and was accepted at the university. The brothers were reunited in June of 1803. Wilhelm, like his father and older brother, chose to study law.

Jacob and Wilhelm had many of the same classes together. One of their favorite professors was Friedrich Karl von Savigny, a young law teacher who often quoted poetry in class. Savigny appreciated the Grimm brothers' love of learning and developed a strong friendship with them. He invited them into his home, where they spent time in his large library filled with medieval literature. One of Jacob's favorite books was a volume that included German song lyrics from the **Middle Ages**. The songs emphasized German pride, honor, and heritage. He read the book more than twenty times because the lyrics were "in a strange German that I only half understood."[4] It was in Savigny's home library where the professor taught Jacob and Wilhelm the importance of becoming careful researchers and thoughtful scholars.

Studying in Paris

In 1804, Savigny went to Paris to conduct research for a book on Roman law in the Middle Ages. It was a large project, and he asked Jacob to help him at the French national library. Though Jacob hated the thought of leaving Wilhelm again, he was thrilled to travel to a city and library so rich in history. Jacob was twenty years old when he arrived in Paris in early 1805. He immediately began reading and copying ancient manuscripts Savigny needed for his book. In his spare time, he explored the wonderful collection of books and manuscripts. He was amazed when he found the original manuscripts he had seen printed in the book of German songs back in Sa-

As university students, Jacob (left) and Wilhelm began to develop an interest in ancient literature.

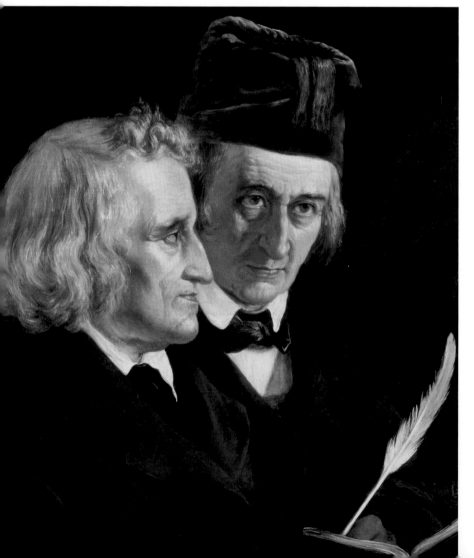

vigny's Marburg library. Jacob loved his time in Paris. By then he realized he had found his true calling—studying ancient literature.

Meanwhile, Wilhelm's interest in old literature was also growing. When he was not studying at the university, he was leafing through books looking for interesting German tales. Like Jacob, Wilhelm was drawn to poetry that reflected the proud history of their homeland. The brothers communicated their love for literature in letters until Jacob returned to Marburg after ten months of research in Paris with Savigny. The brothers eventually moved to Kassel, where their mother now lived with the other four children. The entire family was living together again for the first time in seven years. Though it seemed like old times, trouble was brewing. Napoléon's armies were expanding and conquering many parts of Europe. Much would soon change in the lives of the Brothers Grimm.

Chapter 3

Grimm's Fairy Tales

With war looming, the kingdom of Hessen-Kassel established a war office. In January 1806, Jacob became a clerk in the office. He was pleased to be able to offer money to his mother at last, though it was not very much. He made just 100 **talers**—the equivalent of 70 U.S. dollars—for the year. Unfortunately, his work duties did not make up for what he lacked in salary. His main task was copying letters and other papers. The job was boring compared to the work he had done in Paris with Savigny. He was required to wear a powdered wig and a stiff uniform with a high collar. The only thing Jacob liked about the job was that he could read his beloved books when he finished all of his work.

Jacob's responsibilities at the war office began to change after French soldiers invaded the territory of Hessen-Kassel on November 1, 1806. Napoléon, now emperor of France, immediately established new order. He appointed his brother, Jerome Bonaparte, to be king of the old Hessian territory, which was renamed Westphalia. Kassel became the capital of Westphalia, and the royal headquarters for the new king were based there. The old Hessian war office in which Jacob worked was converted to a supply department for the French armies. Fluent in French, he was asked to continue working in the office. Jacob accepted, though it was a difficult time for him and all fellow Hessians. Their proud culture was

In 1807 Napoléon appointed his younger brother Jerome (pictured with his wife) to be king of Westphalia.

being stripped away. They were forced to speak in French only. And they watched helplessly as Napoléon's soldiers removed books, paintings, and other German artifacts and carried them off to Paris.

An Impressive Collection

Life grew much darker for Jacob and Wilhelm. In May of 1808, Dorothea Grimm died suddenly at the age of 52. Dorothea had long been the foundation of the family, and the six children were devastated. Jacob, who was 23 years old, immediately became head of the family. However, he had already left his job, and Wilhelm, though graduated with a law degree, was not yet employed. The brothers did earn a small amount of money for writing articles about literature, but the family was basically without income. Luckily for the family, Jacob was offered the position of librarian at the royal library in Kassel. His salary was ten times what he had made at the Hessian war office. Suddenly, the family's financial worries were over.

Wilhelm eventually joined him at the library, and the brothers worked side by side at the same desk. It was an ideal job for the Grimm brothers. They were able to research and copy old German folk songs and fairy tales when they were not tending to their regular duties. Some of the stories were ones their mother had told them when they were young. The stories' subjects included goose girls, kings, soldiers, and woodsmen. By writing down the stories, the brothers were preserving a part of Germany's proud history that eventually may have been forgotten.

The Grimm Brothers' Search for Stories

Baltic Sea

North Sea

Germany

POLAND

Berlin

Hanover

Elbe River

Halle

Hoxter

NETHERLANDS

Kassel

Marburg

Hersfeld

Rhine River

Fulda

Steinau

Frankfurt

CZECH REPUBLIC

Hanau

IUM

UXEMBOURG

FRANCE

Danube River

Munich

- ◇ Birthplace of the Brothers Grimm
- Places the Grimms traveled in search of fairy tales
- ◆ Other cities
- — Current border of Germany

SWITZERLAND

LIECHTENSTEIN

AUSTRIA

Pictured is the title page of Wunderhorn, a book of German folk songs compiled by Clemens Brentano (top) and Achim von Arnim (bottom).

While working at the library, Jacob and Wilhelm met friends of Professor Savigny's named Clemens Brentano and Achim von Arnim. The two men shared the brothers' love for ancient German literature. Brentano and Arnim were working on a book of folk songs called *Wunderhorn* and asked the brothers to contribute something from their collection. Jacob and Wilhelm were thrilled to trade several of their folk song lyrics for some they had never seen. *Wunderhorn* was a success with literary intellectuals. The German people living under French occupation also loved the book because it reminded them of better times. Being a part of the book put the brothers on the path toward fame.

Getting Published

Jacob and Wilhelm began to focus almost exclusively on collecting fairy tales. They felt it was their national duty to preserve these treasured stories for all Germans to enjoy. Some of the stories came from handwritten manuscripts that dated from the 12th century. Many had missing pages or were so poorly written they could not be read. So, it was a challenge to restore them. Many of the brothers' fairy tales did not come from manuscripts, but were instead collected from the minds of storytellers.

Among Jacob and Wilhelm's most valuable sources for stories was a nanny and housekeeper from Kassel named Marie Muller. The brothers affectionately called her "Old Marie." She told Wilhelm the story of "Little Red-Cap" (or "Little Red Riding Hood"), a tale about a little girl who goes to visit her sick grandmother and is confronted by a wolf. The following excerpt from the story demonstrates how the brothers quickly turned a seemingly loving and gentle scene into one that terrified readers:

"Oh! grandmother," [Little Red-Cap] said, "what big ears you have."

"The better to hear you with, my child," was the reply.

"But, grandmother, what big eyes you have!" she said.

"The better to see you with, my dear."

"But, grandmother, what large hands you have!"

"The better to hug you with."

"Oh! but, grandmother, what a terrible big mouth you have!"

"The better to eat you with!"[5]

Another trusted storyteller was Katharina Dorothea Viehmann, who had a gift for remembering old tales. Wilhelm collected more than twenty stories from her before she died two years later. Viehmann's most famous story, "Cinderella," evolved from a French tale called "The Little Fur Slipper." An interesting change happened when the story was translated from French to German. The French word *vair*, or "fur," is similar to the

This illustration from "Little Red Riding Hood" shows the wolf getting ready to pounce on the young girl and devour her.

In this engraving (right), the Brothers Grimm listen as Katharina Dorothea Viehmann shares her stories, including "Cinderella" (below).

French word *verre* for "glass." As a result, the fur slipper in the original story somehow became glass in the Grimms' version.

The brothers often **bartered**, or traded, for stories. Viehmann preferred rolls and butter in exchange for her stories. Meanwhile, an elderly soldier named Johann Friedrich Krause swapped some of his stories for some of Jacob and Wilhelm's old pants.

In 1812, Jacob and Wilhelm published the first volume of *Kinder- und Hausmärchen*, or *The Children's and Household Tales* (which came to be known as *Grimm's Fairy Tales*). It contained 86 stories, including "Hansel and Gretel," "Little Red-Cap," "Rumpelstiltskin," "Rapunzel," and "Snow White." All 900 copies were sold within a few months. Wilhelm was pleased that families all across Germany were buying the book and reading it to their children. Jacob, however, had wanted the book to be used for more serious purposes—to be read and studied by scholars. "My book was not written for children," he wrote to Arnim in a letter, "though it fills a need for them, and I am glad that this should be so."[6]

Volume Two

Following the success of their book, Jacob and Wilhelm quickly began working on a second volume. Their work was interrupted when King Jerome Bonaparte, who was now facing defeat, ordered Jacob to pack up any valuable German books, manuscripts, and art he could find and take them to Paris. Jacob hated the thought of stealing treasures from his own country, but to disobey the king meant almost certain death. He gathered the artifacts with great sadness and set off for Paris. His route took him so close to the battlefield that he could hear gunfire in the distance. Fortunately, he made it to Paris and back home safely.

Wilhelm continued working as an assistant librarian in Kassel. He devoted much of his time at the library to researching stories for the second book of fairy tales. With the popularity of the first book, he did not have to leave home in search of stories like he did earlier. People

"Snow White" was one of the 86 stories included in the first volume of Grimm's Fairy Tales, published in 1812.

from all walks of life—professors, scholars, writers, and even commoners—traveled to Kassel to tell their stories, in hopes Wilhelm would record them for use in the brothers' next book. In December 1813, Jacob returned once again to Paris, this time by order of the new Hessian king. Leaders from Austria, Germany, Great Britain, Prussia, and Russia were meeting there to redefine their borders as the long war with Napoléon came to an end. It was Jacob's responsibility to translate documents that were submitted by the different representatives. As was always the case when Jacob was away, he missed Wilhelm very much. "If only the Congress were in [Frankfurt], I could visit you once in a while,"[7] he affectionately wrote in a letter. The brothers, who were nearing age 30, were as close as ever.

Chapter 4

A Lasting Legacy

Jacob was still away from home when he received sad news from Wilhelm. Tante Zimmer, Jacob and Wilhelm's beloved aunt who had done so much for them over the years, passed away in the spring of 1815. Jacob was heartbroken when he got the news, and he returned home a few months later to be close to the family. He had been gone for nearly two years. But he had little time to spend with Wilhelm before setting off once again for Paris. This time the Hessian government, now under German control, sent him to Paris to recover their lost art treasures. Jacob detested the job. Many of the old German paintings and manuscripts were being kept in the same Paris libraries he had visited earlier while doing research. Jacob often angered librarians he knew well by sending the German artifacts back to his homeland.

Earlier that year, the second volume of *Grimm's Fairy Tales* was published. Fans of the first book eagerly purchased the second one, though it did not enjoy the success of the first volume. This bit of bad news did not keep the brothers down for long. They had already set

Published in 1815, the eagerly awaited second volume of Grimm's Fairy Tales did not sell as well as the first.

their sights on other book projects that would make them even more famous.

German Legends and *German Grammar*

While Jacob was in Paris, Wilhelm researched, wrote, and published *German Legends*. The book was an odd mix of stories about dragons, ghosts, giants, and were-wolves, as well as counts, peasants, and soldiers. In one

"The Pied Piper of Hameln" was one of the more famous folk tales Wilhelm published in his book German Legends.

of the most famous stories in the volume, "The Pied Piper of Hameln," Wilhelm tells how a man saved the town of Hameln from rats by luring the rodents into a river by playing his flute. When the town refused to pay him as promised, he led the town's children into a cavern while playing his flute, and the children were never seen again. Wilhelm wrote the story based on an ancient plaque in Hameln. It tells how a mysterious man marched 130 children out of town in 1284, and the children were never found.

When Jacob returned home in 1816, Wilhelm convinced the director of the royal library to hire his older brother as full-time deputy director. It was a selfless act, because Wilhelm was qualified for the job. Working with his brother again was more important to Wilhelm than anything else. The brothers began a long and happy partnership together behind the same library desk. Soon Jacob began researching a huge project—recording the history of German language and grammar. Entitled *German Grammar,* the book of **philology** took Jacob four years to write. The huge volume detailed how languages had changed over the centuries and how they were currently related. For example, he wrote about consonant sound patterns as words changed from language to language. The rule, which scholars still use today, is called Grimm's Law. *German Grammar* became more successful than either volume of *Grimm's Fairy Tales.* It soon made Jacob one of the foremost philologists in the world. He quickly began working on a second edition, which was published two years later.

Wedding Bells

Jacob and Wilhelm's passion for language and literature left them little time for other things, especially courtship. The brothers remained single as they neared age 40. But that changed for Wilhelm in May of 1825. He married Dorothea Wild, daughter of the Kassel druggist. The brothers' close relationship changed very little after the marriage. Wilhelm and Dorothea invited Jacob to live with them. The brothers took morning and afternoon strolls together through the Kassel streets, where they discussed ideas for future books. In the evenings, the brothers joined the rest of the family for dinner. Tragically for Wilhelm and Dorothea, they lost their firstborn

Their deep love for language and literature helped establish the Grimm brothers as renowned philologists and folk-tale collectors.

son, Jacob, to illness in 1826. The couple later had two more sons, Herman and Rudolph, and a daughter they named Auguste. Jacob adored the children. He never married, so he loved and cared for the children as if they were his own.

More changes soon occurred in the brothers' lives. In 1829, the head librarian died and Jacob applied for his job. Wilhelm then applied for Jacob's position. Prince William II, ruler of the kingdom of Hessen-Kassel, refused the promotions. He instead offered a small raise in their pay. Feeling snubbed by the offer, the brothers took jobs at the Gottingen University library in the kingdom of Hanover. Wilhelm worked in the university library, while Jacob became a professor of philology. Wilhelm was later promoted to professor of German poetry. The brothers received several honors for their work at the university.

Meanwhile Ernest Augustus, who was English and an uncle of Queen Victoria, became king of Hanover. He installed a new constitution that took away many of the people's rights and freedoms. Jacob and Wilhelm, along with five other scholars and teachers, rejected the new constitution and swore loyalty to the old one. The Grimm brothers and five others, who became known as the Gottingen Seven, were banished from the kingdom in 1837. Jacob and Wilhelm moved back to Kassel.

The End

Living in exile did not keep Jacob and Wilhelm from publishing more editions of *Grimm's Fairy Tales*. They also began working on one of their last great projects together, the

German Dictionary. The project caught the attention of the king of Prussia, who paid the Grimms to come to Berlin in 1840 to complete the dictionary. Jacob worked on volumes *A* through *C* while Wilhelm was given the task of completing volume *D*. The project took up most of their time, though they did manage to travel frequently.

The brothers spent the next several years working on the dictionary. By 1854, however, they had published only the first volume, *A–Biermolke*. Jacob announced that neither he nor his brother would ever finish the dictionary, and he was right. Wilhelm's health began to fail over the next several years. He finally passed away on December 16, 1859. He was 73 years old. Jacob died four years later on September 20, 1863, at the age of 78. It took 100 years for others finally to finish the dictionary.

With the deaths of Jacob and Wilhelm Grimm, the German people lost two of their favorite sons. The brothers' popular books did not go out of style as a result. The

first volume of *Grimm's Fairy Tales* continued to sell very well, becoming the second most popular book in German history behind the *Bible*. Many of the brothers' tales were translated into other languages so the entire world could read

Jacob and Wilhelm spent their last years collaborating on a monumental project, the German Dictionary.

To this day, Brothers Grimm tales of princes and princesses, heroes and villains, continue to capture the imagination of children the world over.

them. Some stories were even turned into animated movies and are now classics, including Walt Disney's *Cinderella* and *Sleeping Beauty.*

Today, nearly 150 years after Jacob and Wilhelm Grimm's deaths, their old tales are still very much a part of the literary world. They will forever be known around the world as the "Fairy Tale Brothers" as new generations of children open their books and become lost in the world of make-believe.

Notes

Chapter 1: Once Upon a Time
1. Quoted in Donald R. Hettinga, *The Brothers Grimm: Two Lives, One Legacy.* New York: Clarion, 2001, p. 20.

Chapter 2: Leaving Home
2. Quoted in Murray B. Peppard, *Paths Through the Forest: A Biography of the Brothers Grimm.* New York: Holt, Rinehart and Winston, 1971, p. 10.
3. Quoted in Peppard, *Paths Through the Forest,* p. 11.
4. Quoted in Hettinga, *The Brothers Grimm* p. 44.

Chapter 3: *Grimm's Fairy Tales*
5. Jacob and Wilhelm Grimm, *Grimm's Fairy Tales.* Borders group: Ann Arbor, MI, p. 142.
6. Quoted in Hettinga, *The Brothers Grimm,* p. 78.
7. Quoted in Hettinga, *The Brothers Grimm,* p. 91.

Glossary

artillery: Weapons such as cannons, guns, and rockets that are used against an enemy in war.

bartered: Traded something in exchange for a desired object or commodity.

curriculum: A set of courses offered by a high school or university.

Hessians: Native peoples of the German kingdom of Hessen.

lady-in-waiting: A lady who lived in the house of a queen or princess and waited on her.

magistrate: A government official who set forth and kept the laws.

Middle Ages: A period of European history that started about A.D. 500 and ended about 1500.

nursemaid: A person who is hired by a family to look after the children.

philology: The study of language used in literature.

pneumonia: A potentially fatal disease of the lungs caused by infection.

talers: German silver coins used between the 15th and 19th centuries.

turret: A small, ornamental tower.

For Further Exploration

Books

Brothers Grimm, *Favorite Fairy Tales.* Mineola, NY: Dover, 2001. Twenty-one fascinating fairy tales selected from the more than 200 stories composed by Jacob and Wilhelm Grimm.

Wilhelm Grimm, *Grimm: The Illustrated Fairy Tales of the Brothers Grimm.* Berlin: Gestalten Verlag, 2003. A colorful collection of 23 illustrated fairy tales, featuring "Cinderella" and "Hansel and Gretel."

Robert Quackenbush, *Once Upon a Time! A Story of the Brothers Grimm.* New York: Prentice-Hall, 1985. A humorous, illustrated biography of the Brothers Grimm that explores their wonderful tales and fascinating lives.

Jack Zipes, *The Complete Fairy Tales of Brothers Grimm.* New York: Bantam, 1992. Includes over 200 of the Brothers Grimm's best tales, including 40 that are printed in English for the first time.

Web Sites

Grimm Brothers @ NationalGeographic.com (www. nationalgeographic.com/grimm/index2.html. Select a Brothers Grimm tale by clicking on story topics. Includes twelve popular fairy tales.

Grimm Fairy Tales.com (www.grimmfairytales.com/ en/main). Read a brief biography of the Brothers Grimm, watch an animated fairy tale, play games, and more in this fun, interactive Web site.

Index

Picture Credits

Cover photo: © SuperStock, Inc.
akg-images, 30 (top), 35
© Austrian Archives/CORBIS, 18
© Bettmann/CORBIS, 38
Bridgeman Art Library, 7, 11, 26 (lower left)
Corel Corporation, 13
Hulton Archive/Getty Images, 26 (upper right)
Image Club, 9, 29, 30 (bottom), 32, 36, 41
© Bob Krist/CORBIS, 10
Library of Congress, 15
© José F. Poblete/CORBIS, 17
Réunion des Musées Nationaux/Art Resource, NY,
    23
Suzanne Santillan (map), 25
Snark/Art Resource, NY, 26 (large image)
© SuperStock, Inc., 20, 25 (inset photo), 40

About the Author

Raymond H. Miller is the author of more than 50 nonfiction books for children. He has written on a range of topics from U.S. presidents to Native Americans. He enjoys playing sports and spending time outdoors with his wife and two daughters.